Get in the Game! With Robin Roberts

BASKETBALL THE RIGHT WAY

The Millbrook Press
Brookfield, Connecticut

The author and publisher wish to thank Bill Gutman for his research and writing contributions to this series.

Published by The Millbrook Press, Inc.
2 Old New Milford Road
Brookfield, Connecticut 06804
www.millbrookpress.com

Cover photograph courtesy of Steve Fenn/ABC and Superstock

Photographs courtesy of Duomo: pp. 1 (© 1995 William Sallaz), 6 (© 1997 Darren Carroll), 10 (© 1995 William Sallaz), 16 (© 1994 William Sallaz), 43 (© 1997 Chris Trotman); Patrick Flynn: p. 4; © David Young-Wolff/Photo Edit: pp. 8, 29, 39; © Icon SMI: pp. 13, 18 (both), 21; Allsport: pp. 15 (© Otto Greule), 31 (© Todd Warshaw); © WNBA Enterprises, LLC/Bill Baptist: pp. 25, 35; © SportsChrome USA/Steve Woltman: pp. 26, 40

Library of Congress Cataloging-in-Publication Data Roberts, Robin, 1960-
Basketball the right way.
p.cm. — (Get in the game! With Robin Roberts)
Includes index.
Summary: Discusses the fundamental skills of basketball—dribbling, passing, shooting, and rebounding; understanding the team concept; dealing with difficult situations; and more.
ISBN 0-7613-1409-1 (lib.bdg.)
ISBN 0-7613-1285-4 (pbk.)
1. Basketball—Juvenile literature. [1. Basketball.]
I. Title.
GV885.1 .R62   2000   00-025350

CONTENTS

Introduction

Sports have always been a big part of my life. From playing sandlot football with the other kids in my neighborhood in Biloxi, Mississippi, to playing tennis in high school and basketball in college, to working in sports broadcasting at ESPN, I can't imagine my life without sports. It used to be that girls who played sports were labeled "tomboys." These days, however, women and sports go hand-in-hand in so many ways.

Sports can increase a girl's confidence and help her to feel good about herself, and can help her suc-ceed in nearly every aspect of life including school, a career, and relationships with friends and family.

With **Get in the Game!** my goal is to share my love and knowledge of the world of sports, and to show just how important sports can be. What you can learn on the field, court, rink, and arena are ways to solve problems, communicate with others, and become a leader. No matter what your skill level, if you learn all that sports can teach you, how can you *not* succeed at life in general? And the best part is that, like I have, you'll have fun at the same time!

—Robin Roberts

The exciting, skillful basketball played in the WNBA is one of the reasons for the game's booming popularity, especially with girls. Here, superstar Cynthia Cooper of the Houston Comets goes up for a spectacular shot in a game against the Los Angeles Sparks.

What Is Basketball the Right Way?

Ever since its invention in 1891, basketball has been considered an American game. Its popularity, however, became worldwide in the last part of the twentieth century. It's possible that basketball could take the place of soccer as the most played sport in the world.

In the United States the game is thriving at many levels, from town and church leagues to junior-high and high-school programs to the college level and right into the pros. The best players in the world now compete in the National Basketball Association (NBA) and Women's National Basketball Association (WNBA). The brand of basketball that women are playing in the WNBA has often been called the best in the world.

There are those who feel the caliber of NBA play has become poorer in recent years. Many players, though not all, are no longer as skilled in the basics of the game. The players are bigger and stronger than ever, but rely too much on long, three-point shots or crowd-pleasing slam-dunks. The women's game, however, seems more like pure basketball. These players excel at the fundamentals of the game and show off their

skills time and again. For example, the passing is crisp, the women use a variety of shots, and players, whether playing offense or defense, are more team-oriented. There is no doubt that the women of the WNBA play the game the way it was intended to be played.

Playing basketball correctly, however, means more than being able to dribble, pass, and shoot. It also means remembering that basketball is a *team* game. All the players are important, from the top star to the last person on the bench. In order to win, everyone must work together. Playing a team game also means getting along with your teammates, listening to your coach, following directions, and always giving 100 percent on the court.

This is a book about how to be the best basketball player you can be. It will show you more than just how to help your team to victory. Knowing how to win is important, but knowing how to win, and lose, *well* is even more important. A good sense of sportsmanship and how to be a team player is just as crucial to good basketball as knowing the rules and mastering the fundamentals of the game.

This book will help *you* get ready to play basketball the right way.

No matter what your age or skill level, basketball can be a great game if you know how to play it right.

Dealing With Fundamentals

The fundamental skills of basketball are dribbling, passing, shooting, and rebounding. It benefits every single player on a team to master all four of these skills.

DRIBBLING

A good basketball player is able to dribble the ball equally well with either hand. Point guards like Dawn Staley and Teresa Weatherspoon of the WNBA dribble equally well with either hand and can switch hands in the blink of an eye.

Scottie Pippen, the great NBA star with the Chicago Bulls and Portland Trail Blazers, once spoke for many players when he said, "Nobody knows how hard I worked alone on dribbling and just feeling the ball in my hands." Like most great players, he practiced dribbling with both hands.

When dribbling, the ball should be kept low, never bouncing higher than your waist. A top dribbler will also bend down slightly. The low center of gravity this creates gives the player more control of the ball and makes it harder for a defender to steal it. Fingers should always be spread so that the tips can control the ball. Don't slap at the ball. As it comes off the floor meet it with

your fingertips, but let your hand give slightly. Then push it back toward the floor.

Learning to dribble means practicing over and over again. You must ultimately be able to dribble the ball

Great dribbling form means keeping the ball and your body low and spreading your fingers to help keep control of the ball.

without looking at it. That way, you can see the rest of the court while you're dribbling. You must also practice your dribble moving forward and backward, as well as to the right and left. One good drill is to practice dribbling while wearing a blindfold so you can't look at the ball, only feel it. Another drill to try is bouncing the ball while on your knees. Because there is a shorter distance to the floor, this drill will enable you to get used to the dribbling motion with both arm and hand.

Your coach might also have you dribble in and out of a row of chairs, or in a "figure eight" formation. You will also practice switching hands, using a "crossover" dribble that will enable you to change direction quickly. Today's players can dribble the ball between their legs, behind their backs, and occasionally

through the legs of an opponent. They can dribble with their backs to an opponent and switch hands as they do a 180-degree turn.

The ultimate goal, according to Scottie Pippen, is to reach a point where the ball feels a part of your arm and hand. Dribbling becomes second nature and you are free to concentrate on other parts of your game. This can only come with practice.

PASSING

Crisp passing is the best way to move the basketball and get a player open for a good shot. It is the backbone of a good offensive team.

There are four basic passes that young players should master. They are the *chest* or *push pass*, the *bounce pass*, the *overhead pass*, and the *baseball pass*. Of the four, the chest or push pass is the most

There are five players on the basketball court for each team. The traditional setup is to use a center, two forwards, and two guards. The center is usually the tallest player and should be a good scorer, rebounder, and shot blocker. A forward's job is usually to maneuver under the basket and get in for close shots and rebounds. A guard, on the other hand, is more likely to play farther away from the basket, and should be a good dribbler, passer, and shooter, as well as quick and able to set up an offensive play. No matter what her position, however, a good basketball player is skilled at all of the fundamentals of the game.

commonly used, with the bounce pass a close second.

The chest pass is thrown with the ball held close to the chest, the thumbs behind the ball and close together. To make the basic pass, step toward the target, and push the ball away from your body while straightening your arms. Then complete the pass with a final, sharp snap of the wrist. That final snap will give the pass its power.

The push pass is thrown in a similar way, but uses just one hand. Players can sometimes get this pass off faster than the two-hand chest pass and can throw it in a single motion right off of a dribble. It takes more practice to learn to control the push pass, but it is a technique that will help a player in a fast-paced game.

The bounce pass is often used in heavy court traffic because it is hard-er to intercept than a chest pass. One reason is it generally takes tall players a split second longer to bend down to try to pick it off. A bounce pass should hit the court about halfway to the target. That way, it can be caught at waist level. The pass can be thrown with two hands or pushed out with one hand.

The overhead pass is often used to inbound the ball (bring the ball back into play from out of bounds) or to throw a cross-court pass. It is usually thrown over the heads of the defenders. The ball is held above the head with two hands, fingers spread and the thumbs behind. The throwing motion is similar to the two-hand chest pass, but the arm straightening and wrist snap are done from above the head. The passer should take a step toward the target, release, and follow through.

Although the bounce pass
uses the floor and looks as if it's within reach of opposing players, it is the hardest pass to intercept because it can be difficult to judge the position of the ball at any given moment.

The baseball pass is thrown with one hand in much the same motion that a catcher in baseball throws the ball to second base, for example. The pass should come from right behind the ear. As with other passes, you should be sure to step into the throw. Then let your elbow come through first, followed by a snap of the wrist. On long passes, you will find that by rolling the wrist inward (with your palm facing out), the ball will travel in a straight line. The baseball pass is often used to "hit" a teammate streaking down the court on a fast break.

Good passers must be able to deliver the ball on the run to a moving receiver. To do this well, you must anticipate where the receiver will be when the ball arrives and make sure a defender won't be there first.

A player receiving a pass should always keep her fingers spread and hands close together. That way, the ball won't go right through. Watch the ball until it is nearly in your hands, and let your hands give a bit as soon as the ball makes contact. Then draw the ball in close to you so it can't be slapped away and stolen. If you think there is a chance a defender will intercept a pass coming to you, take a quick step toward the ball, which will enable you to catch it a split second sooner.

A good passing team is a pleasure to watch. When the ball moves crisply from player to player, the result will often be an open shot or an easy layup.

SHOOTING

To be able to score, a player must be able to shoot. Young players should master two basic shots: the *layup* and the *jump shot*. The layup is the

A layup is the shot

**most likely to go in because it's
made closest to the basket and
uses the backboard to bounce into
the hoop.**

easiest shot to make. It is made
from close alongside the basket and
is nearly always banked in, or
bounced, off the backboard. All
players should be able to make a
layup from either side of the basket
and with either hand.

The shot is made with one hand
as the player jumps toward the basket. A player going in for a layup
from the right side will push off with
her left foot and take the shot with
her right hand. From the left side,
it's just the opposite. Eventually, you
can practice more difficult layups,
such as going under the basket,
turning, and shooting from the other
side of the hoop. With any layup,
always try to look at the spot on the

backboard where you want to put the ball to bank it in.

The other basic shot is the jump shot, or jumper. Players use the same technique when shooting jumpers from all parts of the court. All jump shots should be taken with the player squaring her body to the basket. As you begin to shoot, hold the ball with both hands (one hand will be used to shoot the ball, the other as a guide), bend your knees, and then start your jump. At the same time, raise the ball just above your forehead with your shooting hand behind the ball with fingers spread and elbow slightly bent. The nonshooting hand should be on the side of the ball and will serve to guide it through the shot.

The ball should be released at the top of your jump. Remove the guide hand and keep your eyes focused on the rim. Just before you

"Following through" with the hand and arm motions used to make a jump shot helps to boost the power and accuracy of the shot.

shoot, your upper arm should be parallel with the court, your forearm perpendicular to the court, and your wrist cocked back. The shooting motion involves straightening your forearm, then flexing the wrist and letting the ball roll off the fingertips. Be sure to follow through by continuing the wrist motion to

its completion, rotating the palm outward.

That is the technique for the basic jumper, but form and style vary from player to player. With practice, you'll find the way that is most comfortable for you.

The free throw, made when a player has been fouled, is released the same way as the jump shot. Most players, however, do not jump when taking a free throw. They relax, bend their knees slightly, then release the ball as they straighten their knees. Shooting free throws takes a great deal of concentration because all the attention is on you.

REBOUNDING

Rebounding is the act of grabbing a missed shot and controlling the ball for your team. A defensive rebound occurs when a player gets the ball after an opponent's missed shot. An offensive rebound takes place when a player gets the ball after a team-mate's missed shot. A team that can "control the boards," or get the important rebounds, will have a big advantage in a game.

Rebounding involves timing, positioning, and "boxing out" other players. A rebounder must jump as high as she can, timing it so that she will reach the ball at the very top of her jump and with her arms extended high over her head. Since no two shots come off the rim the same way, rebounders must learn to anticipate just where the ball will be when the shot is missed.

Being in position means being in the right spot on the court to be able to grab the rebound. As soon as a shot goes up, a good rebounder tries to get to the spot where she thinks the ball may come down. She has to be quick because getting

Rebecca Lobo

(#50) of the New York Liberty works with a teammate to grab a rebound.

The player in the center

is using the technique of boxing out to prevent her opponents from making the rebound: Her arms and legs are spread, and she is crouching low.

good position means cutting or slid-ing in front of opposing rebounders. You cannot push an opponent out of the way. That is a foul.

Once you are in this position, an opponent cannot push *you* out of the way, and you will often have first chance at the rebound. The act of getting in front of an oppo-nent and not letting her get a chance at the rebound is called "boxing out." To keep an opponent boxed out you should spread your feet and arms and get down low. That way, the player behind you can only get the rebound by jump-ing over you, and that, too, often leads to a foul.

You should always try to grab a rebound hard and with both hands. When you come down, opposing players are going to try to take the ball from you or "tie you up." Therefore, you should keep the ball high over your head (especially if you are tall). That will make it easier for you to pivot and throw an over-head pass. You can also bring the ball down to chin level, holding it tight and with your elbows out and away from your body. This, too, will enable you to protect the ball while deciding to either pass or dribble out yourself. The faster you begin moving the ball, the better chance your team will have to get a good shot before the defense can get back and set up.

Dribbling, passing, shooting, and rebounding are the fundamental skills of basketball. There is, howev-er, much more to the game than the fundamentals. A good player also knows about teamwork, winning and losing, listening to advice, and deal-ing with various pressures. With an understanding of all these things you will be on the road to becoming a complete player.

Understandng the Team Concept

Sometimes young players forget that basketball is a team game. Some are more interested in the number of points they can score. Others are worried about playing time, whether they will start the game or sit the bench. Some don't take training seriously and are in less than top physical condition. Still others might become lazy or cynical when the game isn't going their way.

No player with any of these traits is going to be a good teammate. Attitude is every bit as important as fundamental skills.

BEING READY TO PLAY

No player in the world can expect to play a brilliant game from start to finish every time. Some days, it will seem that the basket is as big as a hula hoop. Nearly all your shots go in, and you feel you can't miss. Other days, however, the basket will seem to have a lid on it. But even on a day when your shooting is off, you can find other ways to help your team.

One way you can always help is to be in tip-top physical condition. That means training hard and going all out in drills and in practice. It

also means getting the proper rest and eating right. At some point in your basketball career, this may mean making some sacrifices. You may have to miss a party, for instance, or a day at an amusement park with friends, if it interferes with practice time or with getting enough rest for a game. These sacrifices may be tough to face, but the reward will be the experience of playing for a team where all the players are trying their best and working with each other to be successful.

Understanding the team concept

means staying in the best physical condition you can, and working hard in practice. Not only will these things help improve your individual skills, they will benefit the whole team.

During the season, you need to find a routine that will keep you in peak physical condition. Basketball is a fast-paced game that requires a great deal of running and changing direction. If several key players on a team get tired in the final minutes of a close game, chances are the other team will win. So, every player must work to make sure she can go at top speed for as long as necessary.

Being physically fit is only one piece of the puzzle. You must also be mentally ready to play. Playing any sport well takes a great deal of concentration and mental toughness. If something bothers you, such as a problem at home or at school, it can keep you from concentrating on the game. But you won't help your team if your mind wanders. That's where mental toughness comes in.

A player has to work at shutting out all distractions while out on the court. Try to look at the game as an opportunity to step out of your problem for a little while. Rather than focusing on that tough exam the next day, which could distract you and in turn increase your chances of making a mistake, focus on something you love: basketball and performing to the best of your ability.

TEAM CONCEPT — OFFENSE

Most of the time, offense is a team effort that involves all five players on the court. Occasionally, if a team has an outstanding individual offensive player, it will run a play whereby that person is isolated with room to go one-on-one against a defender. Most of the time, however, the offense must function as a unit with all players working together to make good scoring opportunities.

A team can use many different offensive patterns. Each coach will

create an offense to make the best use of the players available. If a team has an outstanding center who can score close to the basket, the offense may be designed to get the ball inside as often as possible. If a team has an outstanding jump shooter, the offense will be designed to get that player open for a shot.

Most offenses are based on almost constant movement. An offensive player must know where to be on the court at all times. What the team does on offense will also depend on how well the opposing defensive team is playing. All the offensive players will have to be prepared to work even harder to overcome a well-played defense.

At times the entire team will not play well. When this happens, you've all got to try to come together and not give up. Even if you feel you are too far behind to win the game,

you should still try to play better in the closing minutes. You may start to find the magic once more, and it can carry over to the next game.

If you, as an individual, are not playing well, you've got to think about the best way to help your team. Suppose you average 18 points a game, and are one of your team's high scorers. Suddenly, you are having an "off" night and can't seem to make a shot. In a game like this you are better off trying to set up another player who is having a good shooting night. Tell your coach, and see what she thinks. If she tells you to relax and keep shooting, then try your best. If she agrees and tells you to pass more, do that. There are more ways than one to help your team win. If you are having a bad offensive game, try to take your defensive game to another level.

TEAM CONCEPT — DEFENSE

Because the object of basketball is to put the ball in the basket, some players tend to forget about defense. A player may feel that if she made eight to ten shots a night, then she had a great game. But if that same player is just standing around on defense and letting players go around her, then her team is likely to lose. A good player must play team basketball on both offense and defense. In fact, most great teams in history have been great defensive teams. As with offense, all five team members must work together on defense.

A player in a defensive stance has her feet spread apart with one slightly in front of the other, knees bent, with the weight on the balls of her feet. That way she can move quickly in any direction. She should also keep her hands out to the side and low, palms out and fingers spread, ready to bat away or intercept a pass.

Basketball teams usually play one of two basic defenses: the *zone defense* and the *man-to-man defense*. In a zone defense, each player covers a specific area of the court. She will guard any player who comes into that area, but won't follow when the player moves out of that area. Man-to-man defense requires each player to guard a specific opponent and stay with her no matter where she goes on the court. Zone defense is not allowed in professional basketball but is used everywhere else.

In the tougher man-to-man defense there is more running and more movement. Both types of defense, however, rely on quickness and hustle. A defender's job is to try

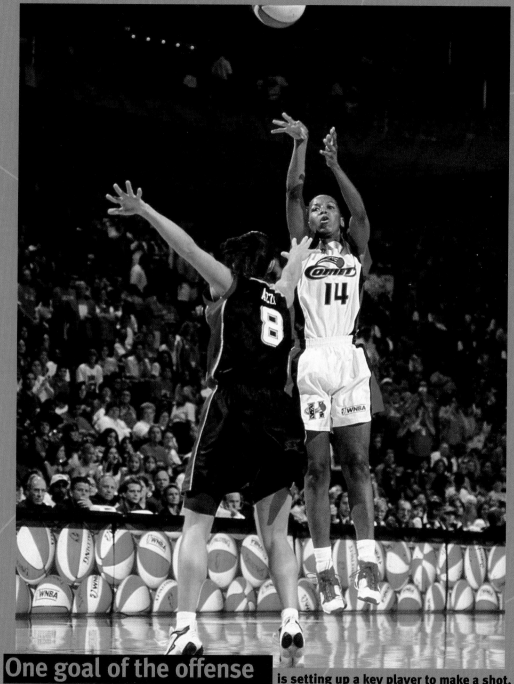

One goal of the offense is setting up a key player to make a shot.
As you can see from this picture, the Comets' offense has done its job
since ace shooter Cynthia Cooper is all but open for a great jump shot.

Dee-fense!
Due to the great defensive form of the Tennessee player, the player with the ball has a big obstacle to get around in order to make a pass or take a shot.

Each player must fully understand the defensive strategy her team is using. Players have to help each other by talking on the court, sometimes telling teammates what is happening behind them. If you get too far away from the opponent you are guarding, you must quickly call for help and switch with a teammate. It may be faster for a teammate to pick up and defend the player you were guarding than for you to move back into your original position. You then slide over and guard the opponent your teammate has left.

to prevent her opponent from getting the ball or getting open for a clear shot. She can also try to intercept a pass or steal the basketball from the dribbler.

Defense takes hard work. Being in shape, having desire and determination, and working with your teammates will make you a force at the defensive end. A strong defense can help a team as much as scoring 20 points on offense can.

Relating to Your Teammates and Coach

Playing basketball the right way also means having the respect of your teammates and respect for your coach. You must be aware of and sometimes overcome a number of things if you are going to relate well to your teammates and coach and be an asset to your team. This is not always easy.

Let's face it: You may not like everyone on your team. Most school and some town league teams consist of the best group of players available, not a group of good friends who happened to join the team at the same time. In addition, there are times when a player and coach won't see eye to eye. A good coach can be a teacher, motivator, and friend. That doesn't mean the coach will make it easy. Some push their players very hard so that the team can be the best it can be.

Both players and coach must learn to compromise at times because the team always comes first. To make compromise happen, you sometimes have to put aside

your feelings. A stubborn player who refuses to listen, compromise, and change might not be on the team for long, no matter how good she is.

WORKING WITH YOUR TEAMMATES

When you're first learning to play basketball as part of a team, the game should be pure fun. You're still learning the basic skills and concepts of team play and shouldn't be too concerned with winning or losing. As you get older, pressure to win will be greater, and that is when problems can occur among teammates. It is then that a player has to put aside her personal feelings for the good of the team.

Maybe you dislike someone on your team. Once you are on the court you have to look at her as a teammate, not as a person you don't like. Suppose, at a key moment in the game, that person is open for a shot and you have the ball. Are you going to pass it to her for the shot, or look the other way? If you think of the team first, you pass the ball.

If you are on the same team as someone you don't like or who doesn't like you, you must find a way to overcome the situation. Make a point to talk to that player. Tell her that even if you can't patch up your differences off the court, both of you are part of a team, and it is important for you to work together. If you are trying to make it work but your teammate is not, you may have to talk to the coach. Don't run to the coach with every little problem that comes along. However, if you can't solve the problem yourself and it is hurting the team, then it is time to see the coach.

As players become older, the problems are often of a different

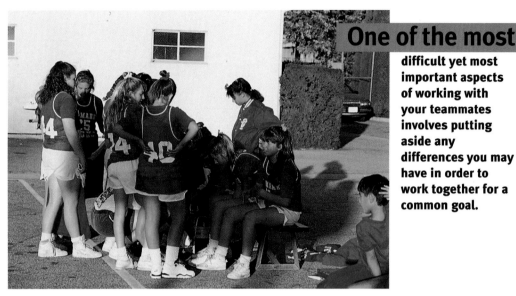

One of the most difficult yet most important aspects of working with your teammates involves putting aside any differences you may have in order to work together for a common goal.

nature. There may be a player who is so competitive that she constantly urges her teammates to play better. This kind of encouragement can be positive if it isn't overdone.

Conversely, the use of insults, name-calling, or even dirty looks can be detrimental to the team. Never yell at or insult a player for making mistakes. If that player is giving 100 percent, then the team should make the best use of her assets and try to play around her weaknesses.

An assistant head coach at Stanford University, Amy Tucker says that the ability to get along with teammates is an important quality she looks for when recruiting players. "A positive attitude with teammates is something I always look for. If I see a player in high school yelling at her teammates or coach, that is usually a bad sign."

When you are part of a team, there is no room for personal grudges or a me-first attitude. That can make it difficult for a player to get along with her teammates, and in the end can only hurt the team.

WORKING WITH YOUR COACH

Basketball coaches come in all shapes, sizes, and styles. No matter the style of yours, the coach is the boss. You may not always agree with the coach's methods, but while you are a member of the team you have to try to work it out the best you can.

For younger players, the coach should be a teacher and a motivator. There should be no pressure to win or lose. Unfortunately, some coaches feel they have to be tough and yell at their players. A very young player, however, should never be yelled at—this can discourage an athlete and make her want to leave the team and possibly not play at all. If a young team has a coach who is always yelling, the players can try talking to the coach as a group. If that doesn't work, the members of the team should talk to their parents or school administrators. Instead of yelling, it is usually more beneficial if the coach tries to explain to players why he or she is angry, and discuss what they can do together to change the situation.

Many high-school and college coaches may be under pressure to win. This kind of pressure can make coaches at this level drive their teams harder. There is nothing wrong with that as long as communication between players and coach remains strong.

For example, always tell your coach if you have an injury that might limit you in practice or in drills. If the coach orders you to work through it, you could make the injury worse. Tell the coach you prefer to see a trainer or doctor before continuing. A good coach will permit this.

Coaches should be trusted leaders. They have the ability to teach their players more than just the fundamentals of basketball. They can instill values and a sense of sportsmanship that go way beyond the basketball court. Many college and professional athletes who have found success after completing their sports careers have cited one or more of their coaches as a positive influence and role model in their lives.

Some coaches, by their nature, are yellers and screamers. They yell when the team isn't practicing well. They sometimes yell after the team loses a game. They yell at a player if she makes a key mistake. They yell

Not only can a good coach help you develop your basketball skills but she or he can also be a trusted guide and mentor.

instructions from the bench during a game. Sooner or later, almost every player will have a coach who yells a lot. At higher levels of competition, it isn't necessarily a negative thing.

If a coach balances yelling with teaching and also complimenting players for a good play, then it isn't so bad. If she yells after a loss, but then takes time to explain how to correct the mistakes, that's okay, too. If she yells and pushes players in practice, but the team is in better shape than its opponents the last five minutes of a game, it isn't such a bad thing. In these cases, yelling is just part of a good coach's style.

However, if the coach yells and berates the team, and never compliments anyone, then it isn't so good. If the coach's yelling takes the form of personal insults to individual players, that is wrong. If a coach has a problem with a player, she should speak to that person privately. Conversely, if a player is having a problem with a coach, she should speak to the coach privately. Most problems can be worked out if those involved speak openly about them. In the end it is getting encouragement and having the feeling that the coach cares that make both players and team better.

Dealing With Difficult Situations

Anyone who plays basketball with organized teams for a number of years is going to run into some difficult times. It may be pressure from home, or from teammates. It may be problems with a coach, or with your own game. It may be a bad mistake that you cannot forget. You may feel that you aren't playing enough or that your teammates can't keep up with you. All these things will test your character and your love of the game. You've got to handle them with maturity and good common sense.

SUDDENLY, YOU AREN'T PLAYING ENOUGH

This is a situation that many players face as they get older and begin playing at the junior-high and high-school levels. At the beginning, everyone gets to play because learning the game and having fun are the most important things. Later, when winning becomes more important, the best players get the most playing time.

Many players are bothered by this. It is sometimes difficult to accept the fact that someone else may be better than you. The easy way out is to complain, to say that the coach is not being fair, and that you should be playing more. Some players will even go so far as to quit the team.

There are better ways to deal with this problem. First, work hard and be ready. As a substitute, you never know when you will be needed to play. A starter may be injured or foul out of the game. Suddenly, your team is depending on you to take up the slack. If you play well off the bench, chances are you will begin to get more time on court. In the meantime, accept the coach's decision and continue to work at improving your game.

If you do these things, you will earn the respect of your coach, teammates, and friends, and no one will ever call you a quitter.

YOU CAN'T FORGET A MISTAKE YOU MADE

Your team is losing by one point with the clock ticking down. You have the ball, but don't have a good shot. Suddenly, you see a teammate cutting to the basket. All you have to do is pass her the ball for an easy layup, but you throw the ball a split second late and it goes behind your teammate and out of bounds just before the buzzer sounds. You will probably leave the court feeling that your mistake has cost your team the game.

It is important that you learn to let go of mistakes. If you cannot forget your mistake, chances are you will tighten up the next time or maybe even freeze and not be able to make a play at all. Don't let one mistake overshadow the half-dozen good things you did in the same game.

Remember, one player doesn't cause a team to lose a game. If you miss the last shot and your team loses by one point, think of all the other missed shots. Mistakes are made during an entire game. As a player, you should learn from your mistake, forget about it, and play on.

YOU CAN'T SEEM TO CONTROL YOUR TEMPER DURING A GAME

You can be an intense competitor and still keep your cool. Top players let their talent speak for itself. If a referee's call goes against them or a teammate makes a mistake, they accept it and play even harder.

If you argue every call that goes against you, you might get a technical foul, which will give your opponents one or two free throws and the ball back again. Too much arguing will even get you ejected from the game. This can hurt your team and possibly cost them the game. If you lose your temper with teammates, you will also lose their respect. This often divides a team, making it harder to work together.

Teresa Weatherspoon
is a tough, intense defensive player who shows her emotions on the basketball court. But she knows how to avoid letting her emotions get the best of her and interfere with good sportsmanship.

If a call goes against you and you feel ready to explode, take a deep breath and think about what is best for your team. You cannot help your team from the locker room or by drawing technical fouls because of your temper. Even if a player on another team starts trash-talking or pushing you, walk away. She may be thrown out of the game and you'll still be playing for a win.

YOU ARE THE STAR OF THE TEAM AND CANNOT TOLERATE THE MISTAKES OF OTHERS

The superstar athlete sometimes has problems of her own. If she is a fierce competitor and very talented, she may be a perfectionist. This can make it difficult for her to accept the mistakes of others. Even if a great player finds herself on a mediocre team that is not winning, she cannot take it out on her teammates, especially if everyone is playing hard.

The first few years he was in the NBA, Michael Jordan played for losing teams in Chicago. He just kept working, playing as hard as he could, and, finally, the team got new players who joined with him to build a winner. If you are a star player, do the same thing. Improve your game, play your best, and try to help make the players around you better.

You may encounter other dilemmas as you continue to play basketball. If you work to overcome them, you can. At times, you may need a word from a coach, a friend, or your parents to help you through. The important thing is that you love the game and enjoy playing. If you lose the joy of being on the court and being part of a team, then you may also lose everything else the game can give you.

Getting the R*ight Advice*

People always have something to say. It's no different in sports than in other activities. A basketball player will get advice from many different people—parents, coaches, teachers, perhaps even a girlfriend or boyfriend. Not all this advice is good advice. A player who follows bad advice can hurt herself or her team. By the same token, good advice is not always what a player wants to hear. The trick is listening to some-one you respect and learning to sep-arate good advice from bad.

Even those who mean well can sometimes give bad advice. Think about the following statements:

- *You're better than she is. You should be starting, not sitting on the bench. I wouldn't take that if I were you.*

- *You need to play better than that. If you don't get a basketball scholarship, there's no way you can go to college. Your whole future might be riding on the next three games.*

- *You ought to be taking more shots. The team is losing most of its games, but you could be the league's scoring champ. I made a bet with someone that you would win it.*

- *Why go to practice today? We're all gonna hang out and listen to some great music. Everyone wants you there. Tell the coach you don't feel well or that you have a test to study for.*

These are examples of bad advice for basketball players. That doesn't necessarily mean that the people who gave it had bad intentions. Not everyone understands sports, and some people don't realize the things an athlete must do for her team.

Now contrast those statements with the following, positive advice that many players receive:

- *I know you're not happy about being on the bench. Still, stay ready, work hard, and your chance will come.*

- *If you get a basketball scholarship, that will be great. If not, we'll find another way to help you go to college. Just keep your grades up and enjoy your last year in high school. Remember, no matter what happens, we love you.*

- *I know you feel awful about missing that last shot, but think of all the positive things you did out there tonight. If another chance comes to take the last shot, take it. You're a good shooter.*

- *Hey, we'd all love to have you at the party tonight, but the game tomorrow is really important to the whole team. There will be other parties, but the team is counting on you tomorrow.*

Most basketball players are fortunate enough to have good, supportive coaches. Players who don't, however, may hear well-meaning friends and family encouraging them to quit the team or give up basketball altogether.

It can be tough for parents to see their daughter not get as much game time as they think she should. But the bench is a very important part of every successful team, and it's just as important for nonstarting players to be as fit and ready to play as the starters.

Young people are often open to all kinds of suggestions, and bad advice can often lead an athlete to make a bad decision. Parents, especially, influence a young athlete by the advice they give.

In addition, parents should not act as if their daughter's basketball games are the most important events in their own lives. The athlete is not playing to satisfy the expectations of parents or friends. She is playing for her own enjoyment and for the team's success. A young athlete in this situation should try to understand that parents usually have their daughter's success and best interests in mind, and aren't really aware that what they're saying is not helpful. Supportive parents who are aware of these potential problems and work to avoid them are the best allies a player can have.

As a young basketball player, you will get advice from all directions. Being able to distinguish the good advice from the bad is just as important as being able to hit a jump shot with the game on the line.

A Few Words About Winning and Losing

Sports and good sportsmanship go together, with much of it revolving around knowing how to win and lose gracefully.

WINNING

Many people feel that sports today place too much emphasis on winning. Certainly, at the professional level in all sports, the objective is to win. There is no greater satisfaction for a pro athlete than to be part of a WNBA, World Series, Super Bowl, NBA, or NHL championship team.

But has the emphasis on winning in professional sports trickled down too far? Is there a win-at-all-costs mentality even in elementary school? Usually, at that level, it depends on the attitude of the coach. Winning should not be the only reason you begin to play basketball.

Certainly, there is enormous satisfaction when you play well and your team wins. To win a championship at any level is the ultimate. It is something no player ever forgets.

A player who can lose with grace and dignity is often called a good loser. One who can win with the same qualities is definitely a good winner. Imagine the success of a whole team made up of good losers and winners!

How you win, however, shows not only the kind of player you are but also the kind of person you are. The trash-talking player who is constantly playing "in-your-face" games with her opponents and then has a *we're the greatest* and *I-told-you-so* attitude when her team wins is not a good winner.

A bad winner is no better than a sore loser. If you gloat over a victory, your opponents will not only lose respect for you, but they also will play harder to beat you the next time. Chances are that many of your teammates won't like it, either. There is nothing wrong with showing elation after a great play or great shot, or certainly when your team wins. However, you should not rub it in the faces of your opponents.

If you are lucky enough to be on a winning team, make the most of that opportunity. You can savor the moment without being mean-spirited. That's the mark of a true winner.

<black bar heading>
LOSING

No one likes to lose. It's simply not as much fun as winning. A player doesn't have to be told that. She feels it, almost from the time she begins playing the game. Some losses hurt more than others (a very close, hard-fought game; an important league game, a championship game, a game against close rivals), but none are fun. Even a superb individual performance doesn't have the same satisfaction if your team winds up on the short end of the score.

There is nothing wrong with working to win and wanting to win. No team, however, wins all the time. Being a good loser is certainly as important as being a good winner.

By contrast, being a bad loser is a tag that a player cannot easily escape.

What is a bad loser? A bad loser is a player who begins complaining as soon as her team is behind and appears to be losing. She may grouse at officials and berate her own teammates if they make a mistake. A bad loser begins to show the body language of losing: moping around the court, looking down at the floor, maybe mumbling under her breath. At some point, she may even stop trying, not playing her best because the game seems lost.

Some bad losers will even look for a physical confrontation. They begin to play dirty, fouling hard, giving opponents a little extra push. On occasion a player will lose her cool completely and throw an elbow or a punch. This is the worst kind of loser of all.

A bad loser is a player who does not shake hands or congratulate the winners when the game ends. A loss can hurt badly, but it's important to show this type of respect after a hard-fought contest.

The best cure for losing is to win the next time out. As a productive member of a losing team, you should rally your teammates around you and vow to win your next game. Losing should bring a team together, not break it apart. Remember, everyone is hurting after a loss, not only you. The "good loser" always tries to turn a negative into a positive. She learns from her mistakes and tries not to make them the next time. She works harder and tries to help make her teammates better. By knowing how to lose and being a good loser, you are ultimately becoming a winner.

Basketball can help you to live a healthy lifestyle, give you discipline, teach you to be part of a team and work for a shared goal, and teach you lessons that can be used in other areas of your life.

Above all, basketball should be fun and give you a great deal of satisfaction. But that will happen only if the game is played the right way. That means mastering the fundamentals, learning to accept responsibility, keeping yourself ready to play, making necessary sacrifices during the season, working together with teammates and coaches, and learning to win and lose with grace.

If you can do those things, you'll be playing basketball the way it was meant to be played, and you will enjoy your entire basketball career, whether it lasts two or twenty years, or more.

Get in the Game!

There are many ways to get information on the fundamental skills and the other elements that go into playing basketball the right way. Here are some books and Web sites to get you started.

BOOKS

The Art of Basketball: A Guide to Self-Improvement in the Fundamentals of the Game by Oscar Robertson with Michael O'Daniel (Oscar Robertson Media Ventures, 1998).

Basketball by Thomas S. Owens and Diana Star Helmer, Game Plan series (Brookfield, CT: Millbrook, 1999).

Basketball for Boys and Girls: Start Right and Play Well by Bill Gutman (Tarrytown, NY: Marshall Cavendish, 1990).

Basketball Fundamentals by Sidney Goldstein, Nitty Gritty Basketball series (Philadelphia: Golden Aura Publishing, 1998).

Teresa Weatherspoon's Basketball for Girls by Teresa Weatherspoon and Kelly Whiteside (New York: John Wiley & Sons, 1999).

WEB SITES

www.jes-soft.com/playbook/index.html
  This site includes plays and drills, with available software to download

www.knowledgehound.com/topics/basketba.htm
  This site has links to tutorials, and includes coaching tips, practice drills, techniques, rules, and more.

www.sportsforwomen.com/news/just_hoops.html
  This site contains women's basketball news, including the National Collegiate Athletics Association (NCAA), WNBA, and international reports.

www.wnba.com
  The women's pro league home page

Index

Page numbers in *italics* refer to illustrations.